CLOUD BLUNT MOON

Chris Mulhern

Published in the UK by IRON Press,
5, Marden Terrace, Cullercoats, North Shields,
Tyne and Wear NE30 4PD. Tel: 0191 253 1901

ISBN 0 906228 46 8

Distributed by Signature Book Representation,
Sunhouse, 2 Little Peter Street, Knott Mill, Manchester M15 4PS.
Tel: 0161 834 8767 Fax: 0161 834 8656 Email: signatur@dircon.co.uk

First published 1994
Second Print 1995
Third Print 1998
Copyright © Chris Mulhern 1994

Printed in England by Peterson Printers, South Shields.
Design and typeset by Unlimited Images.
Illustrations by Lesley Oakley.

northern
arts
PROMOTING THE ARTS
IN THE NORTH

for Rebecca

I'd like to thank:
Peter Mortimer at Iron Press,
Lesley for her artwork,
Dave for design and typesetting,
and all three for their patience.

I'd also like to thank the editors
of the following magazines
in which many of these poems
first appeared:
The Haiku Quarterly
Bare Bones
Blithe Spirit -
(Journal of the British Haiku Society)

CONTENTS

NEW MOON

spider
silvered
morning

last night's rain
cupped
in an upturned leaf

clouds...

wisps

of

white

dis-

solv

-ing

bee lazily

drifts
on the whim
of a breeze

gypsy girl

lifting
her skirt
from the hedge

rain - laden
hawthorn bows
heavy with scent

crow flaps into
the down-bowing
branches

the shape - changing
twilight
deepens...

in the powder blue sky
a faint sickle,
turning silver

moon maiden

she looses
her robe

which
falls

silk-silvery
cool

to her feet
and

steps out
naked

first love:

catch
in her breath
her snagged heart seeps

THE CRESCENT

the old town

that
early evening
sunlight

turning
the sandstone
golden

through narrow streets
a reed flute,
wavering

stoop - dropped - coin

flute to her lips
she smiles
her thanks

a little later

twilight
descends

tinting
the spaces

night itself
will fill

smooth...

creaky
bare wood
staircase

one hand
sliding
the rail

shutters flung wide
to the fragrant
night

breathing in deep
the scents
of your hair

a silky film
softens
the crescent

- tang
of licked
scent

entering...

your eyes
close
around me

the crescent
and her shadow
complete

in each other's arms

sleep comes
gently
breath by breath

FIRST QUARTER

sunlight

seeping
through half - shut
blinds

and dreams
sliding back
into sleep

early morning kiss :

all warm
and fuddled
with sleep

morning sunshine:

even
the caged birds
singing

bougainvillea

sheets
billowing
from balconies

spilling
the fragrance
of flowers

fat Mama

flaps - a - rug
from her window

big lungs
filling

the morning
with song

iced - coffee

a cool dark
tongue
exploring ...

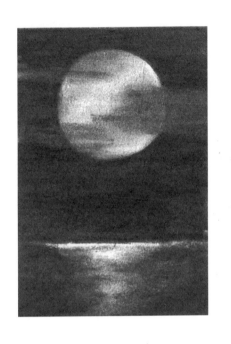

FULL MOON

early morning :
virgin wet
sand sheen

the bubbles
left
after the wave ...

She stands
a little
        plump

in the shallows
lapping
        her ankles

floral - skirt
bunched
        in her hands

a child
        beginning

down on the beach

stick figures
sling stones
at the sea

on the waters
a pale grey calm

the sun has set
and yet, the sad

sweet ache
remains

my love
hugging
her legs

her tides
no man
can understand

Full Moon

beneath
her path

on the silvery
seas

the silent
shoals

slide
by

WANING

lovers silence :

where branches end
and reflections -
begin

sensing
the stillness:
a leaf trembles

53

breeze
in the treetops
murmurs of change

clouds
scudding over - the peaks
hidden

deep in the mountains :

the cavernous
crumbling
of thunder

blackbird
leaves - a branch
waving

glossy black beetle
slips under
a leaf

plash

on the grey
ash

- phalt
burst

the first
full

berries
of the storm

LAST QUARTER

in full rush -
the storm

ceased

tinkling, trickling
away

in the after - silence :
a stunned
calm

she glides clear
of the cloud
- and is gone

DARK OF THE MOON

left at dawn :

dewdrops
on grass - blades
five tears to a stem

cow track
the good mud
squelches

swift - whipped - wings

crow
passing low
overhead

the wood :
leaf - still

familiar paths
but
all has changed

your absence :
an ache
- always with me

"Cascadences
of thrush - song"
- poem of the darkening wood

thin thread of smoke
drifts
over the trees

- gypsy camp

somewhere, far off

a reed
crying
in the wind

ink
dark
night

a warm thank you
to Nick
and to all of you
whom friendship, curiosity
and that happy haze
of another late night
first persuaded
to read these poems

IRON Press was formed in Spring 1973, initially to publish the magazine IRON which more than two decades, and more than 1,500 writers on, survives as one of the country's most active alternative mags – a fervent purveyor of new poetry, fiction and graphics. £12.00 gets you a subscription. Try our intriguing book list too, titles which can rarely be found on the shelves of mega-stores. Fortified by a belief in good writing, as against literary competitions or marketing trivia, IRON remains defiantly a small press. Our address is at the front of this book